Fessenden!

Looking Back on a Small-Town North Dakota Life

Carol Owen Reynolds

Fessenden! Looking Back on a Small-Town North Dakota Life
Carol Owen Reynolds
Published February 2026
Heirloom Editions
Imprint of Jan-Carol Publishing, Inc.

Graphic Design by Tara Sizemore

ISBN: 978-1-970471-22-9
Library of Congress Control Number: On file

You may contact the publisher:
Jan-Carol Publishing, Inc.
PO Box 701
Johnson City, TN 37605
publisher@jancarolpublishing.com
www.jancarolpublishing.com

This book is dedicated to the people of Fessenden, ND,
and to my brother, Nate Owen.

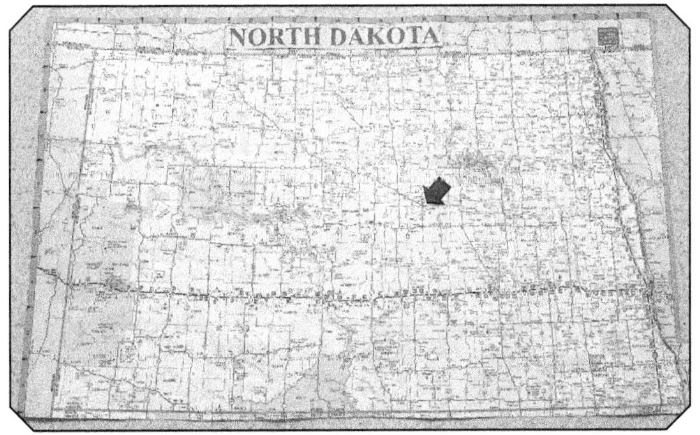

Also by Carol Owen Reynolds:

Holy Land Journal 2016

The Locas: A Collection of Stories about 13 "Crazy Women"

Stories from a North Dakota Cheerleader

Table of Contents

Grandpa & Grandma

"We never really grow up;
we only learn how to act in public."
— Paraprosdokians

It's my feeling that we don't truly appreciate our grandparents until later in life or until they are gone. I was so lucky to have known my grandparents on both sides of my family.

Mom, Emma, was from a family of 12 children, all reared near Fessenden and Heaton, North Dakota. Mom ran away, across a field, to marry my dad. Her father tried to catch her, but by that time he was crippled and couldn't run as fast as his daughter, who was a track champion. In the days before they called it "track," it was called "play day," and she had won several medals for her speed. Mom stayed with my paternal grandparents until the wedding.

Mom's mother, Maggie, came to the United States from Germany, although Ancestry shows that I have only 6% Germanic ethnicity. Grandpa Kahler was also said to be German. He said his parents were German, but he was born in the Black Sea area of Russia. He told me his family had gone to Russia to teach the Russians how to farm.

We laughed, because in later years when he visited San Diego and his kids decided to visit Tijuana, they told him to tell the border agents he was born in the United States. He said, "I was not. I was born in Russia and I'm proud of it!"

Grandpa and Grandma Kahler lived on a farm near Heaton. Grandpa Kahler was also a hunter between North Dakota and Canada, so he had several guns. Grandma would not allow the guns to be brought in the house. He once set his shotgun heavily on the front porch by the kitchen door. It blew a hole in the roof of the porch.

Grandpa Kahler also had cattle and horses. He had trouble with thieves stealing his horses, so he set a bear trap in the barn where the horses were tied. The next morning, he found a man's hand in the bear trap!

We visited Mom's parents often after they moved to Tuttle, North Dakota. Before we could play with our other cousins, we had to stand in a line in front of Grandpa Kahler, shake hands with him, and tell him our name and who our parents were.

Grandma Kahler was a fastidious housekeeper. So much so, that she wouldn't go to bed even if there was one dirty cup in the kitchen. She would heat the water, wash the cup, rinse it, dry it, and put it away before bedtime.

Grandma Maggie would make what we called "head cheese." When my uncle would butcher a pig, he would bring the head of the pig to Grandma Maggie. She had him set the head on a chair in the enclosed front entry porch. She would go to work, thoroughly scrubbing it, removing the skin, and scraping the fat down to the bare bones of the head.

I may have missed a step or two in her process. I had to stop watching her because I thought what she was doing was gruesome. I know Grandma would boil the jars for the head cheese and fill them with the fat. I couldn't even try eating the head cheese after watching her process it. It was eaten on crackers or bread.

My father's parents were born in Wisconsin, and again on Ancestry, they tell me I'm of English, Welsh, and Northwestern European ethnicity. Grandpa and Grandma Owen lived just a couple miles from us on their farm near Fessenden.

Grandma Elizabeth was intelligent and could play the piano by ear. She could hear a song at church, then go home and play it on the piano. She had three children: Ruby, William (Bill), and my dad, Newton (Newt). Grandpa Pierce left Grandma with the children the first winter after they moved from their home in Wisconsin to North Dakota. He had returned to Wisconsin to retrieve their personal belongings and furniture. She and the children slept on the floor and used dried cow piles for fuel that winter.

Grandma Elizabeth stepped into a much different life with Pierce. Somehow, she was strong enough to survive prairie life, but a tornado hopping across the prairie toward their farm was a bit too much for her. She had not seen one in Wisconsin and stepped out on the front porch to see what everyone had said was so scary. She watched it for several minutes and kept raking her hand through her hair. Several days later, the spot on her forehead hair turned white. The white streak stayed on her hair until the rest of her hair turned gray when she aged.

I don't remember Grandpa Pierce ever saying one word, although I'm sure he did talk from time to time. It seemed all he ever did was work. They owned three quarters of a section of land, and during harvesting, he worked from four o'clock in the morning until 10 o'clock at night.

Mom said Grandpa Pierce called Grandma Elizabeth "Lizzie." Aunt Ruby lived with Grandpa and Grandma Owen. She was the driver and we called her "The Bubick." Grandma Elizabeth liked to visit us at our farm because Mom made great desserts, especially lemon and apple pies. When we saw them coming down the road, we'd yell, "Hey, Mom, the Bubick is coming!"

Mom and Dad sometimes had to go places on business or places kids couldn't go, and we were left with Grandpa, Grandma, and Aunt Ruby. They were the most loving of anyone to us that I can remember. Unfortunately, we didn't see it that way in the beginning. Nate and I screamed and tried to follow our parents out the door. It usually took several minutes for us to settle down. We could have anything we wanted to eat, and Grandma would read us stories. We could take a nap with her. By the time our parents returned, we weren't ready to go home.

The Windmill

"There is no security between the cradle and the grave."
– *THINK AGAIN* BY ROBERT ANTHONY

Life on the farm, six miles east of Fessenden, was better suited for my brother, Nate, than for me. I was allergic to almost everything around me and I tried to keep up with him. Poor Mom! She had her hands full, trying to keep up with all the work assigned automatically to a North Dakota farmer's wife, including keeping the lanterns filled with kerosene, because we didn't have electricity. Later, we were able to have electricity brought to our farm and proudly displayed a yard light.

During the summer, the work for Mom was quadrupled with harvesting crews to feed three times a day. She also took a morning snack and coffee to the men in the field. She baked bread and cinnamon rolls for the harvesting crew. After the cinnamon rolls were formed and put in the pans for baking, she would pour the fresh cream directly from the brew she took from the separator in the kitchen.

It's no wonder that the crews loved to work for my dad. Who would ever get a freshly baked cinnamon roll, dripping with cream, anywhere else? How many places served steak and eggs for breakfast?

A few years later, I found some "ration books" in a drawer and asked Mom what they were. She said that during the war (World War II), food was rationed, even to babies, to give everyone an equal share of of food.

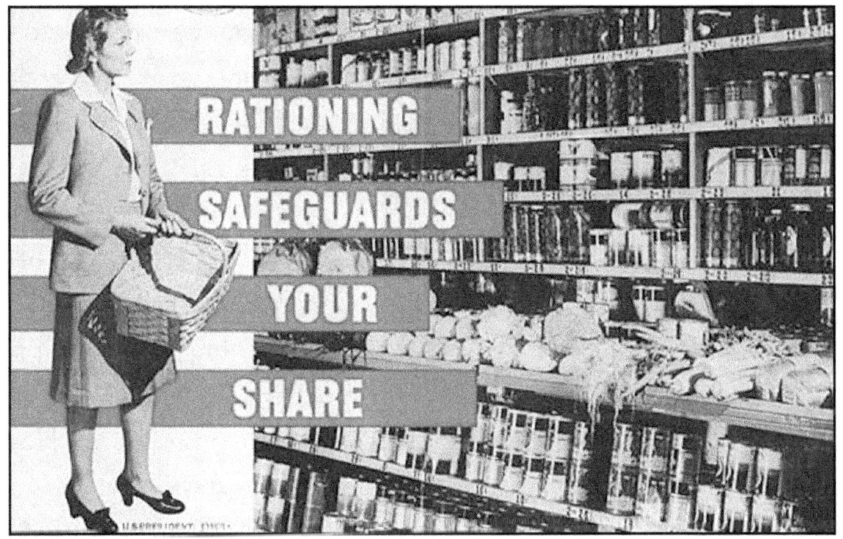

She exchanged her farm products with others to get coffee, sugar, eggs, and flour rations because she needed these products to feed the harvesting crews.

The summer *during harvesting season* when I was just eight months old, Nate and I got whooping cough! He was two and a half and was able to throw up in the cup Mom gave him, but I still didn't have the sense to hold the cup and catch the vomit. I'd just lie there and let the vomit run all over me. Sometimes, I now think back and wonder how Mom kept going during those times.

At that time, there was little that could be done for my asthma attacks, other than avoid the many places on a farm that made me sneeze, my eyes swell, and me gasping for air. Several times, I wandered off into the wheat field and Mom found me by listening for the sneezing.

When I had an asthma attack, Mom would lay me on the kitchen table and cover me with cold washcloths. I don't remember this being a good treatment, but I suppose I enjoyed the attention.

It seemed safe enough on our farm for the two kids. Sometimes, I lost my shoes in the field and "shoe searching" interrupted Mom's busy

day. I would run back to the house whenever the rooster chased me, and he would peck at my ankles.

Nate tried to copy all the things it took to be "one of the men" who worked on our farm. At age four, he could pretty much cover any of the available space on our farm. He was warned to stay off the road and was taught what was ours.

Windmills marked every farm, and their blades drew the water from deep below the earth. Summer storage at the well bottom was a good place to keep butter, milk, and other farm products cold. The storage was limited but good for these products until we needed them or took them to the creamery in Fessenden for sale. There were metal steps up one side of the windmill, making it easy for any needed repairs. Sometimes one of the men would climb to the top just to have a look at the countryside or to see if we were getting welcome company from town, since we had no telephone at that time.

Because Nate liked to be "one of the men," he decided it was his turn to climb atop the windmill and see what was so darn interesting up there and the surrounding area. It was the place where only the men could go. It was their place and now could be his place, too. Kind of scary, but he knew he was old enough, at age four, to try climbing up to that special place only the guys could go.

It took Nate a long time to climb the windmill because he had to stop on each step to catch his breath. Then, too, the farther up he climbed, fear struck, and he had to decide if he truly wanted to be "one of the men" on his dad's farm.

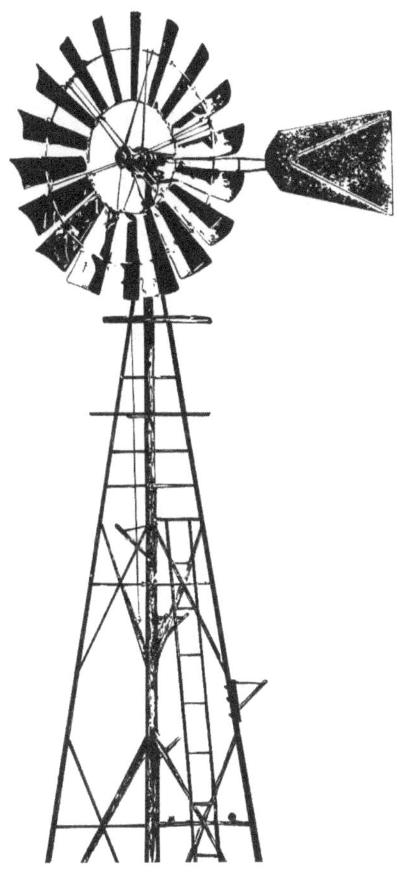

Illustration by my grandson, Alexander

Oh, how rewarding it was when Nate reached the top! He could see as far as where the earth met the sky on that flat North Dakota prairie! He could no longer keep this total experience to himself. He had to share it with someone. It couldn't be his sister, because he thought she was only two and too little and dumb to know the greatest test of his manhood. Mom was the only other person around.

So, he hollered, "Hey, Mom! Look what I did!" She came running outside and couldn't find where Nate was hiding. He hollered again, "I'm on top of the windmill!" Mom froze and clutched her chest. When she recovered from her shock, she calmly said, "Oh, yes, I see. Come on down now." She couldn't bear to watch as he descended the windmill, fearing he would miss a step and fall to his death. She turned and went slowly into the house as if everything was okay.

When Nate proudly reached the bottom of the windmill, he started toward the house, and Mom ran outside. She tore a branch from the nearest bush and slammed it against his skinny butt! Confused, because he didn't understand why he was in any kind of trouble, he held his butt and meandered off to the barn to find his next adventure.

When Dad came home from the field that evening, Mom said, "Before you get a bite to eat, you have to remove the bottom four steps from the windmill!"

The Fire

"If you carry your childhood with you,
you never become older."
– Abraham Sutzkever

To say my brother, Nate, challenged me would be a small exaggeration. He dared me to try and do everything he could do, even though he knew he could do better. I couldn't keep up with him, and because I was two years younger, I was the perfect target to be picked on and teased. Not only that, but we were the only two kids on a big farm, so there were no other targets available to him.

He could slide down the banister. He could chase the chickens and calves. He could hang around with the hired men and the harvesting crew. He was the master of the farm, and he thought I was the short-legged chicken with asthma. Well, I was the one chosen to sit on the porch and churn butter! So grown up!

When I was four, and again during harvesting, Mom would load up the car with the mid-morning coffee and cinnamon rolls for the harvesting crew. The cinnamon rolls were still hot out of the oven and oozed with the topping from the fresh separated cream.

It was hotter than blazes and no air conditioning yet in the cars. The '42 Ford windows had to be rolled down so we could breathe. Nate thought it was "big time" sitting in the front seat. Little did he know,

I rather liked the back seat. When we hit the field, the grasshoppers seemed to be intent on jumping in the car. Nate would sometimes catch one and shove it in my face saying, "This grasshopper is going to spit molasses in your face!"

I'd scream and he'd laugh. Mom had her hands full, getting in the field to serve the coffee and rolls. Everything would have to stop for the mid-morning respite. I hated every part of harvesting, especially this part. Why couldn't I just stay home and play with my dolls?

Mom would hurry home to start the lunch that also had to be delivered to the field. When we got home, I started crying and begging Mom to just let me stay home from the lunch delivery. She said, "I think you are just too young to stay alone, even though you are responsible for your age." I kept begging and following her around the kitchen while she prepared the sandwiches and fresh potato salad.

The pork and beans had to be heated on the kerosene cook stove in the kitchen. Mom had always thrown the stick matches in a small half tin on the lower ledge of the stove and cautioned us to never touch the burned-out matches and to stay away from the stove, especially when she was cooking.

Mom said, "Time to go. We don't want the pork and beans to get cold and the potato salad to get hot!" I begged and cried until she finally consented. I had to promise to stay in the house and stay away from the stove. I promised and kept that promise. I began playing with my doll, Patty. That doll and I had a tight friendship. We could go to many imaginary places and visit our imaginary friends who lived in town at Lucy's house. I wished we lived in town so we could visit for real with Lucy and her dolls.

Smoke began to slowly stir in the small tin on the kerosene stove, but I thought it would burn itself out as it had done in the past. I guess there were too many wood matches in there, and the smoke kept swirling around the kitchen.

I had promised Mom I wouldn't leave the house, but I would not want to be here if the smoke turned to flames. I wasn't about to leave Patty behind, and I needed to save my winter coat because I would need it when the snow came to our farm.

By now, there was a lot of smoke as I ran out the front door and waited on the front porch until Mom and Nate showed up. I left the front door open so the smoke could come out. She rushed past me and smothered the fire in the tin with her apron.

I waited outside until Mom came out, and I apologized for going outside. She said, "You did the right thing. I just have one question. Why are you wearing your winter coat?" I told her I didn't want it to burn because I'd need it when the snow came.

This is actually not the end of the story. Mom had to scrub down the entire kitchen, including the ceiling and walls. I watched her as I colored some pictures at the kitchen table the next day. Mom was thoroughly exhausted, I'm sure. She decided to take a nap the next afternoon after taking lunch in the field to the harvesting crew.

I didn't want to take a nap and told her I would be okay until she got up. I decided to display my pictures on the kitchen chimney wall next to the stove. I couldn't find the paste, but I had heard from an adult conversation that you can make paste with water and flour, so I mixed me up a batch and pasted the pictures to the chimney wall. I did have some trouble pasting them up high, so I had to stand on my old highchair.

I was sure Mom would be surprised when she woke up. I couldn't understand why she got so upset and made me spend the rest of the afternoon in my bedroom. The next day, I had to go along with Mom and Nate to feed the harvesters, like it or not.

The Move to Town

"You are a child of the universe, no less than the trees and the stars; you have a right to be here. And whether or not it is clear to you, no doubt the universe is unfolding as it should."

– MAX EHRMANN, "DESIDERATA"

From the time she was able, Mom had been raised to be a farmer's wife, I think. She did work also at the creamery in town, where farm products were sold. When she was 16, she competed with the other girls who were plucking chickens. They were paid by the chicken, so she was the fastest and made the most money. So when I say, "My mother was a chicken plucker," you can believe it.

Mom was also an advocate for her brothers and sisters to help them get out and on their own. She would let her younger sisters stay with us until they could find work. She saw to it that a couple of her brothers worked for my dad and lived with us until they could get their own place.

My brother, Nate, started school in Fessenden at age six (no kindergarten in those days). He was allowed to ride the speeder, a small railroad handcar that passed by our farm at just the right time of day. I looked forward to the day I could catch a ride in the same way, but Mom just couldn't see me on the speeder with two railroad workers and my brother.

Another problem with living in the country was that we were sometimes "snowed in" and could miss several days of school. Then, too, Dr. Matthai recommended I have my tonsils out before I started school. So, before we moved, Mom made an appointment with St. Aloisius Hospital in Harvey for my tonsillectomy. It was the same hospital where I had been born, 23 miles from the farm.

Mom carefully explained to me just what was going to happen with breathing in the Ether and how I wouldn't feel anything after that for a short period of time. She assured me it would make me feel better; that I would have fewer colds and asthma attacks. And, I'd be closer to my friend, Lucy! We could play with our dolls more often! It all made sense to me.

Mom and I left for the hospital the afternoon before the tonsillectomy. When we arrived, the nurse showed us to my bed. It was a crib! It was in the hallway! Didn't she know I was too grown up to sleep in a crib? I hung my head and tugged at Mom's coat. She looked down at me and said, "The hospital is very crowded, and all the beds are taken. Besides that, it's just for one night." I needed to know this so we could move to town, and I'd be able to start school and play dolls more often with Lucy.

Mom helped the nurse undress me and put on my pajamas. Then, Mom helped me get into the crib. She patted me gently on the rear and said, "Do what you're told. I'll be back tomorrow after the tonsils are out." She left.

I remember taking three deep breaths and going to sleep on the third breath. When I awoke, my tonsils were gone. Mom came back after lunch and took me back home to the farm

My parents sold the part of the farm with the house, barn, and outer buildings but kept the acreage that was planted and harvested. They bought a house on the outskirts of Fessenden about two blocks from Schimke's Gas Station. Close enough for Lucy and I to travel back and forth to play with our dolls!

My Poor Leg

"You do not need a parachute to skydive.
You only need a parachute to skydive twice."
— PARAPROSDOKIANS

After we moved to town, my brother Nate and I were sometimes left with Mom when our dad would be gone for a few days. Nate went off with his buddies and they tried to get in trouble without being discovered. Mom always said, "Everyone has to do their part." That meant we each had our duties around the house and yard.

I was still young, only about seven years old, and was being taught to help with dishes and sweeping the floors. Mom knew almost everyone in Fessenden, then a town of about 450 people. We were living on the outskirts of town, across the street from Uncle Bill, Aunt Ida, Marlys, and Beverly. The Reules (we pronounced their name "Riley") were on the same side of the road, and Mom and I would visit them often. I loved to visit them because there were always good desserts to go with the coffee.

Elmer, their son, was friendly and did the chores around the farm and fields. He always teased me and acknowledged me. I liked him and thought he was just a great guy. He always did the milking of the cows at 5 p.m. It was just like clockwork.

It was cold and the snow was about two feet deep. Mom began heating the water to start the dishes and had the music on full blast. I was bored and asked to go outside. She said, "It's really too cold to play outside today, and you could help with the dishes, you know. Besides that, it will be dark soon." I begged her to just let me go outside for a few minutes. I would bundle up and be back inside before the dishes were done.

Mom finally relented and helped me pull up my snow pants and high-top boots. I hurried outside and trudged down the front path toward the road. There was a deep ditch between our property and the road. Across the ditch was a short approach with a large pipe below allowing the water to flow under the approach and giving us access to walk on the road.

Maybe I could walk across the approach and part way down the road, just to see Elmer leave the house and go toward the barn to milk the cows. I wouldn't go any farther for fear that Mom would accuse me of snooping in the life of our neighbors. Just to see him.

My right foot slipped off the approach and sank into the ditch! Quickly, I could feel the ice-cold water filling up my boot. I tried to get leverage with my left foot to pull me back up, and it just didn't work. There was a layer of ice between the water and the snow, and it began freezing around my knee. I screamed for Mom several times, but the radio was blaring so loud, she couldn't hear me.

It was getting dark, and there was no one around on this cold day on the outskirts of Fessenden. No one, *except Elmer Riley*. Oh, God! He was so nice, and I didn't want him to think I was an idiot, but I had no choice. I hollered, "Elmer Riley, Elmer Riley!" Nothing. The ice on my knee was beginning to freeze all the way through my snow pants. Pain. Then I screamed as loud as I could, "ELMER RILEY, ELMER RILEY!"

I saw Elmer running down the road toward me as fast as he could. He hollered, "Hang on, Carol, I'll be right there!" He dug around my knee, careful not to slip in the ditch himself. It seemed forever before he finally got me out of the ditch. He picked me up in his arms and ran to the house, banging on the front door.

Poor Mom. She was confused and ready to scold me when Elmer said, "This girl could lose her leg! She was stuck in the approach a long time and her leg is frozen." We had just heard on the radio that it's best not to put anything hot on a frozen body part and to let your own body temperature slowly unfreeze the frozen part. Mom told Elmer she would try to unfreeze the leg and thanked him for rescuing me. Elmer stayed for a long time until he was sure my leg was okay and that Mom would not need to call Dr. Matthai, our local doctor.

A few days later, Elmer stopped by to see how I was doing and to make sure my leg was okay. He said, "Let's see if that leg is still kicking." Then, he held me by my wrists and ankles, swung me up and down, and landed me on the couch. I screamed with laughter and fell in love with Elmer Riley. That lasted until the sixth grade, when I had a massive crush on a new boy at school.

Crabby Teacher

"If Lucille jumped off a cliff, you'd jump off too!"

– Famous Emma Sayings

The first day of school, Mom gave Nate and me strict orders not to start a fight, but it was okay to defend ourselves. Nate was to hold my hand all the way to the first-grade room. I asked him what I should do if some kid asked me my name, and he said, "Tell them it's none of their beeswax!"

I think Nate's task of holding my hand only lasted that one time. He had his friends to think about. Anyway, it wasn't any fun holding a girl's hand.

The first-grade teacher was a real crab! The rules were strict. We were assigned seats and had no choice about what we liked. Our teacher was someone who Mom called a "Blacksocker," which at the time was identified as a strict religious group that dressed very plain and wore black stockings. She also wore a "rat tail" on her back neckline that was just a rounded cloth with which she wrapped her hair.

This hairstyle was created during the war in factories to keep women's hair from getting tangled in the machines manufacturing war products. Women had begun to work in factories during the war to replace the young men being drafted.

A couple of weeks after the start of school, I told Mom I couldn't see what was written on the blackboard. She had a talk with the teacher, and I was seated in front of the classroom.

Every morning, after the Pledge to the Flag, we had to put our hands on our desk and sit up straight. The teacher went around the room and asked each student if we washed our face and hands, combed our hair, brushed our teeth, and cleaned our fingernails. If we did each of these things, we got a gold star on the chart that was posted on the wall for everyone to see. I loved putting up my gold stars.

The first grade was combined with what was called "2B" and was for kids who were not quite ready for second grade but had learned somewhat more than first graders. The teacher had little patience for some of the kids in 2B but didn't want them back the next year. Sometimes she swatted a couple of them on the head. That method never seemed to help them.

We were told that if we needed extra help, we could ask another student. Lucy was the smartest in our class, so we went to her desk often. It got to be that she had too many people lined up by her desk, so that rule had to stop.

Lucy stuck by me always. We went everywhere together. Even to the bathroom. We played hopscotch and rode the merry-go-round together. She was with me when I was running and looking at her, not paying attention to a boy coming from the opposite direction. He and I hit head on, and I suffered a deviated septum. When I got home and told Mom what happened, she said, "Well, next time, look where you're going."

Everyone liked the slide best, and the boys would fight in line to get ahead of the girls. Nate had listened to Mom and wasn't fighting until he remembered she had told him, "Don't fight, but defend yourself if someone else starts to fight first." He finally socked another boy in line and took his rightful turn. I don't remember Nate ever fighting again, even all through grade school and high school.

Every February there was a Valentine box in every classroom. We bought the Valentines at the dime store (5- and 10-cent store in Harvey), the Gamble's Store, or at Aunt Ida's dry goods store on Main Street in Fessenden. We could put our Valentines to the other students in the box and carefully chose the most appropriate messages to each of our friends.

The Valentine box that year was in the shape of a heart and covered with red crepe paper. It had a white paper arrow that looked like it was going through the box. There was always a drawing for the Valentine box after the holiday, and this year, I won the box! Allen Stock said, "You are a lucky duck!" I worked with Allen during my junior and senior high school years at the *Wells County Free Press*. He later became editor and publisher of the newspaper in Carrington, North Dakota.

I had always fought the battle of being too skinny, and Mom talked about it to Dad's cousin many times when we visited her at her apartment. One time during our visit, she said she had gotten a small cross on a chain and would be willing to give it to me if I drank a glass of milk every day for a month. As much as I hated drinking milk, I did it, and I still have that cross in my jewelry box!

It was so cold in North Dakota during the winter, and we were not allowed to wear slacks to school. Only dresses with snow pants under them. I still had the habit of going without shoes whenever I had a chance to take them off. One morning when it was time to get ready for school, we searched the entire house looking for my shoes. Mom finally gave up and said, "Just get ready and we will go to Ida's store and buy new ones." When I began putting on my snow pants, there they were—inside the legs of the snow pants!

A Nice Teacher

"Going to church doesn't make you a Christian any more than standing in a garage makes you a car."

— PARAPROSDOKIANS

We had the same teacher in second and third grade, and she was the opposite personality of our first-grade teacher. The second and third grades were in the same room, and the same teacher taught both classes. We also had a music teacher.

My brother and his friends had another girl to tease (Lucy). It didn't take long for the boys to set Lucy and me up for pranks. They sometimes told us how things were supposed to be for boys and how they were supposed to be for girls. There were "girls' bikes" and "boys' bikes." The bike riders were never to cross the line.

I memorized "The Night Before Christmas" and gave my memorization at the First Congregational Church on Christmas Eve. I could not have done it without the help of Lucy and her mother, Evelyn. Lucy had given the same piece a year earlier.

During these years, Lucy and Mom encouraged me to attend Sunday school. If I was having a bad day, Lucy would pick me up on her way to church and sometimes even waited until I got out of bed and dressed.

It is my feeling that every child could benefit from Sunday school and be taught right from wrong, no matter the Protestant or Catholic

Sunday school they attend. A chaplain who counseled prisoners once said, "90% of the inmates in prison never went to Sunday school."

Mrs. Lowery and her two boys, Dick and Spike, sat with Mom, Nate, and me at a Congregational Church dinner. Both mothers had taught us how to behave properly and that we were not to be too loud or unruly. Nate and I got into a loud argument about the fact that I had to eat everything on my plate before we could leave, and I started to cry. Then, Dick pulled a hair from his food and hollered, "Look, Ma! A hair!" That was one time Lucy was glad she wasn't sitting with me.

It was in the third grade that both Lucy and I were the last two standing in the Spelling Bee. We were both stumped by forgetting to capitalize "Halloween."

It was around this time that my sister, Candace, was born. Nate and I stayed with Grandma Owen and Aunt Ruby Owen after school when Mom was in the hospital. They had moved to town after Grandpa Owen died. I was eight years older, and Nate was 10 years older, almost to the day. Candace was about the cutest kid you will ever see. I talked about her a good deal in my last book, *The Locas*. She was Loca Numero Seis.

It was also about this time that my parents began divorce proceedings. My dad had become a slave to alcoholism and lost his family in the process. He always favored me over Nate, like the time he took me to the dime store in Harvey and said I could have any doll on the top row of the store. All the doll dresses were pink and there was only one in a blue dress. I picked the one in the blue dress.

Years later, my dad finally sobered up and became his old self again. He died of cancer in his late 50s. Candace and I flew to the funeral from San Diego to Bismarck. I think I came close to the same addiction as my father, but I was saved through a Catholic Cursillo. If you ever have a chance to attend a Cursillo, be sure to take advantage of it, because it could save your life. In the Protestant faith, it is called "Walk to Emmaus."

I became a Cursillo speaker, and it was The Last Talk of the First Day, a personal witness talk. I was helping with dishes in the cafeteria later that day. A lady came in and asked me, "During your talk, did you say something about alcoholism?" I said I had, and she said, "After your talk, my daughter said she would never take another drink in her life!"

Mom gave Nate and me our chores also around this time. Nate was given the job of mowing the front and back yards that covered about an acre of the four acres we had purchased on the outskirts of Fessenden. Our place was adjoining the Wells County Fairgrounds. In the winter, Nate had to keep our long driveway shoveled from the back door all the way to the road.

The other three acres contained a barn and pasture. Mom kept a big garden and always saved a row for her flowers. There were several lilac bushes in our yard. When we were expecting company, Mom would have me cut lilacs for the dining room table.

From the time he was 13 years old, Nate worked at Solberg's Grocery Store and delivered the Minot Daily News on Sunday. Years later, I recalled his custom of shoveling snow off the roofs of elderly people. This was because the snow became heavy and could cause the roofs to cave in. He didn't ask permission and never charged them for the work. He just went from one house to another, of those in need, and did that work.

Mom gave me the task of washing dishes every day and cleaning the house, top to bottom, every Saturday. She said, "Everyone must do their part." She also told me that scrubbing the floor on my hands and knees gave me a small waist. I believed her because I indeed had a small waist.

After I scrubbed the kitchen, I laid newspapers on the floor to keep the floor from getting dirty again. This was my own invention, and she approved.

The Cistern

"The only running water we had
was water we ran after!"
– Famous Emma Sayings

No water could be wasted at our house. My brother, Nate, brought a clean, new cream can of water from Schimke's gas station a couple blocks away on a wagon in summer and on a sled in the winter. We kept it in the covered pail until ready for use. A second uncovered pail of water and a dipper was kept in the pantry for drinking and cooking. The water from the cistern that was pumped into the house by hand was used for bathing, laundry, and everyday use.

Our cistern was basically a deep hole in the ground with cement walls that extended about two feet above ground level. The top was also cement, but a two-by-two feet wooden lid opened the top to fill the cistern with water. Dad had a large oblong tank on top of a long trailer and hauled water from the tower furnished by the City of Fessenden.

A more accurate description of Fessenden would be "town," not "city," because at that time, there were about 460 residents. Some places had wells with pumps, but water towers dotted towns all over the state of North Dakota with names identifying them in big letters. Some water towers still exist and are, in fact, used today.

In the spring, the snow runoff was a good source of water from the ditch west of town. It could be pumped into our tank on the trailer and was actually the purest source of water.

A couple of times before filling, when the cistern was almost empty, Mom thought it should be cleaned at the bottom to remove the accumulated sediment. Remember the size of the lid? Guess who was the smallest and skinniest in the family? Me!

Today, everyone talks about the process. Here was our process:

- **First**, they lowered a pail, an old dipper, and a rag tied to a rope into the cistern.
- **Second**, they tied a rope to MY WAIST and lowered ME slowly into the cistern!
- **Third**, I began scooping up the most water I could and dumped it into the pail.
- **Fourth**, I sopped up the remaining water and sediment with the rag.
- **Fifth**, I tugged at the pail rope, stepped aside a bit, and they slowly hauled up the pail.
- **Sixth**, they hauled *me* up slowly. The reason they hauled me up slowly was because my body would start swinging and they didn't want my head to hit the top of the cistern.

Now, you might ask, "Weren't you scared?" The funny part of it was, I thought that if the house caught on fire, my parents would run away and forget me at the bottom of the cistern! Or, you may ask, "When did you stop cleaning the cistern?" I *disqualified* myself for cistern cleaning by gaining weight.

I took a public speaking class at Grossmont College when I was 64 years old and gave a personal narrative speech about the cistern. I left time open for questions, and the young students just sat there and stared at me as if I had three heads! I'm sure they didn't believe me.

Three Close Calls

"You'll never find a better sparring partner than adversity."
– Walt Schmidt

Nate was gone most of the time with his friends and didn't have time for me, unless he was bored too! He did have a BB gun and a small rifle. He shot gophers, cut the tails off, and sold the tails for five cents each. It was an incentive to lower the population of the gophers and save the crops. Later, he started shooting rabbits. I think he may have gotten approval from the local farmers for shooting the rabbits, but I don't know why.

This was the first close call: Sometimes I got completely bored when Lucy wasn't around. We now had electricity hooked to our house! We were able to buy a refrigerator and didn't have to use the lanterns, except when we went to the barn. Behind the house was a loose wire that nearly touched the ground. I was swinging on it when Mom came around the corner looking for me and trying to find out why she had lost power to the house.

Mom gasped and said, "Stop swinging on that wire and don't touch the end of it! It's a live wire!" It didn't connect with me that I was in any great danger.

I guess you could call this second one a close call: It was when Mom found a mouse in the kitchen. I heard her scream, "Nate! Help me catch this mouse! He's headed for the pantry and will get in the food!" Nate did, indeed, try to help her, but the mouse ran in the pantry anyway.

Then, she yelled, "Shut the door so I can catch him!" Things got worse. The mouse ran up the leg of her slacks. She really screamed this time, "He's caught in my girdle!" Skinny Mom certainly didn't have to wear a girdle, but in those days, lots of women customarily wore them. When she got the mouse out, she stomped on him and killed him! Nate cut his tail off and threw him in the outdoor toilet!

This third close call was the closest: Sometimes Nate and I stole a Camel or Old Gold cigarette from Mom or Dad's pack. They never missed them because they were pretty heavy smokers in those days.

We had plodded out a small area in the wheat field on the adjoining lot between our house and the Reule farm. The lot did not have any structures at the time and was used as a field. The field stretched out of town for a couple miles. It was fall, and the field was ripe for harvesting.

Mom was unhappy with the bedroom wallpaper that had aged and begun peeling. Because the house was old, built in 1889, she decided she wanted the walls plastered. Not too many people knew how to plaster, and she was lucky to find someone to do the work.

The man doing the work was a smoker and left his package of Camel cigarettes on the upper windowsill in the kitchen. After everyone was in the bedroom watching him plaster, Nate reached for the pack and stuck a cigarette in his shirt pocket. He said, "You keep a look out, because I'm going out in the wheat field to smoke this one!" I said, "I'm going along with you." He said, "No, you're not. There's not enough in the pack for both of us. He might notice it!" Then Nate headed out the back door.

I was so angry, I ran right in the bedroom and told Mom, "Nate stole a cigarette and is going out in the wheat field to smoke!" The blood ran out of her face, and she tore out the back door toward the smoking area we had plodded out in the field.

Just as Nate was about to strike a match, she screamed at him, "What the hell are you doing? What's been going on here? Don't you know you could start a prairie fire that would burn for miles and cost farmers thousands of dollars? Are you nuts? Get the hell out of there and go up to your room. I'll deal with you later!" She slapped him across the back of his head as he passed by her. On his way out of the field, he said, "Carol's been smoking here too!"

Mom gave me the dirtiest look I ever saw on her face. I wandered off and didn't talk to anyone for the rest of the day. She was so angry, she told a number of people what we had done and embarrassed us each time. I would have rather had a beating than be so embarrassed. I didn't smoke again until I was 16 years old when Mom said, "If you're going to smoke, smoke at home, not in public." I didn't smoke in public, but a couple of times, I snuck away with Ben Willert and we would talk and have a smoke in his car.

Cheerleading!

"The speed of the leader determines the rate of the pack."

– Wayne Lukas

By this time, Mom had married Elmer Wentz, and I was in junior high (now called middle school). I was getting sure of myself. I thought cheerleaders were the greatest girls in the entire universe. I wanted to be one of them. We had junior cheerleaders and senior cheerleaders. I "tried out" for junior cheerleader in the seventh grade and wasn't chosen. I was devastated but not deterred.

The method of choosing cheerleaders was that there was an assembly of the entire high school (about 125 kids). The principal would line up anyone interested in becoming a cheerleader, stand behind the lineup, and hold his hand over each girl's head. The number of the girls needed for the cheerleaders who got the most applause became the new cheerleaders. In other words, it was a popularity contest (as one of the losers said).

Undaunted, I tried out again when I was in the eighth grade and became a junior cheerleader! We met to discuss what we would wear and order it from the Sears catalog. We were stuck with all of us wearing black slacks because our school was very conservative and girls could not wear slacks to school. Only cheerleaders could wear slacks on the days of our pep rallies. No dresses for cheerleaders.

Then in high school, I was chosen as a senior cheerleader. It was mind bending for me to help decide what we would wear. I had to pay for my own clothes, and I was only making 50 cents an hour at the Wells County Free Press. They called me the Circulation Manager in charge of sending out the renewal notices and taking orders for ads in the paper.

I made small stencils when the renewals came in and stamped them on the top corner of the newspapers. The rest of the papers were delivered to Fessenden and Harvey's Main Street stores.

We decided it was time for cheerleaders to wear dresses when I was a sophomore in high school. Someone would have to "get up the guts" to confront the superintendent and make our case. We would all go in to "make our case." Sharon was chosen to be our spokesperson. She was the best one because she was afraid of no one!

Then she gave our argument about how "all the other cheerleaders in the state of North Dakota wore dresses." We were the only ones who "had to wear slacks." We could wear dresses that had a dropped waist and were softly pleated, so as not to flare out too far and show anything above the knee.

He listened without interruption and then said, "You can wear that kind of dress, and I would like you to get the approval from the home economics teacher. Of course, you will want to wear slacks to the football games because you will freeze to death out there in the winter."

We tore out of his office and jumped up and down in the hall by the second-grade room. Sharon let out a scream of joy and the teacher came out and told us to shut up!

We had a basketball game in a town about four hours away, and the movie *Giant* was playing. We had to kill some time before the game and decided to see the movie. We didn't realize the movie was much longer than most (about 4 hours), and someone from the gymnasium had to come get us. We were late for the game.

There was a State Cheerleading Conference in one of the larger towns in North Dakota that would last a couple days. It was our good fortune to be allowed to attend with the cost being covered by the school district. It was so grown up, we thought, to be able to go and learn new cheers and some tumbling stunts. We couldn't wait to get back to Fessenden and try out some of our new cheers.

The first game night, we did the new cheer we loved the most:

Knock 'em in the backbone!
Sock 'em in the jaw!
Take 'em to the cemetery!
Rah! Rah! Rah!

The next day, the cheerleaders were called to the superintendent's office. He looked at us for a long time, then said, "That wasn't a very nice cheer you gave last night." We were mortified and shamed. We decided it wasn't worth trying any more new cheers this year.

The last year of high school, the cheerleaders sewed tops to just the waistline and could be worn with our slacks or skirts. The skirts didn't have dropped waists this time. No asking the superintendent this year.

We had a set of twins the last year, and we designed a cheer that involved us running ahead, and each twin was to hold my hand on each side as I did a flip. That cheer didn't work out so great, both because they each failed to grab my hand, and I fell on my tailbone! It hurt so darn bad, but I told no one because Mom had taken me out of cheerleading two weeks in the last year when I was having trouble with my periods.

Years later, after I was married, my husband patted me on the butt and asked me what was wrong with my tailbone. I told him I thought it was okay, and he said, "Well, feel mine. It's nice and smooth. Yours is all knotted up!" The next time I went to the doctor, he checked it out and said, "You're lucky it broke outward. If it had broken inward, we'd have to break it again when you have children."

I was nominated by the other cheerleaders in my senior year to give the "Cheerleader Talk" at the Lettermen's Banquet. I asked Mr. Farrington, our editor/publisher at the *Free Press*, what I should say, and he gave me a great suggestion. I said, "I never saw so many people so happy to get an F!"

Encounter at Whiskey Ranch

"There's a fine line between cuddling and holding someone down so they can't get away."

– Paraprosdokians

There was a small grove of trees about a mile and a half east of Fessenden. Lots of teenage kids used to go there and "neck." I wasn't one of them. Not because I didn't want to, but because I was not allowed to go there anyway. After all, "What are people going to think?" The rules at home were very strict and I had learned to live with *or* around them.

Seldom did I go to a movie by myself, and Lucy had the good sense to stay home because it was 10 below zero that night. There was a lot of snow on the ground. Mom said, "Is Lucille going?" I answered, "Why do you always ask me if Lucille is going? What difference does it make? I'm old enough to go someplace by myself."

I paid my 35 cents and couldn't even get a bag of popcorn because my friend, Sandee, had elected to stay home, too, and she ran the popcorn stand. An older boy from school had been at the movie, along with just a couple other people, but I had not spoken to him.

Carol, Lucy, & Sandee

I don't remember much about the movie, except that I told myself after, "My girlfriends not only have the brains to stay home, but it was a lousy movie anyway!" I decided to treat myself to a cup of hot chocolate at the Connor Hotel Café before I started walking the half-mile home. The same boy from school was there, too, but left the café before me.

As soon as I left the café, he pulled up in his car, leaned over, and opened the passenger door side of the car. He said, "How about a ride home?" I hesitated because I had been told not to get into a car with a boy. Then he said, "It's pretty cold out here." I thought, "Oh, what the heck? I'll just have him leave me off at the foot of the driveway. No one will ever know I got a ride home alone with a boy."

He was a nice boy and from a good family. He was popular at school and played sports with my brother, Nate. He had a steady girlfriend.

He passed by my house. I said, "Hey, you missed my house back there." No response. Then I said it again, "I thought you knew where I lived." No answer.

Even after telling him twice that he missed my house, I thought he would turn around and go back. Damn! I was cussing myself for even getting in his car, but I had no control of the situation.

He still did not say one word as he pulled up across the road from Whiskey Ranch on a small approach, and he left the car running. He grabbed me, pulling me to him. He tried to kiss me, and I pulled away and said, "I'll tell your girlfriend!" He said, "I don't care!"

I decided to walk home and thought I could get back to town, even though it was cold and freezing outside. I opened the car door, and it dragged across the deep snow. I knew at that moment I would sink in the snow and never make it back to town.

He sat there staring at me, and I said, "I'm gonna tell Nate!" He said, "Okay." He pulled out of the approach and headed back to town without a word. He dropped me off at the foot of our driveway. Mom asked how the movie was, and I told her it was no good and I stopped at the Connor Hotel Café for a cup of hot chocolate.

That boy and I never said another word to each other for the rest of our lives. When I read his obituary, I saw that he was an upstanding citizen, wonderful husband, and a great father. Also, he was a prosperous and deeply religious man.

I tell you this story not because I want you to think the boys in Fessenden were bad people, but because I want you to know that we learned in Sunday school at the Congregational Church that forgiveness is divine. That you know people can change. Sometimes, they do.

Senior Year

"Take kindly the counsel of the years,
gracefully surrendering the things of youth."
– Max Ehrmann, "Desiderata"

When I was a sophomore, my attitude began to get lousy. Our physical education teacher was a woman of great patience. She was also the home economics teacher and carried a big load of work at the school. I didn't like her. I didn't like having to play touch football with the other girls. My attitude was stinky, and I knew it wouldn't hold out much longer.

Some of the girls found a harmless snake when we were outside playing touch football as part of the physical education class. I picked up the snake by the tail and flipped it high in the air. It snapped end over end and took off across the field. The teacher let out a scream and grabbed me by the arm. She said, "We are going to the principal's office." I knew him well.

The teacher told the principal the whole story, and when she was through talking, she was still shaking. Then she left me with the principal. He folded his arms and turned his back on me for a long time. Then he turned around and looked at me long and hard. He said, "Carol, I don't think you realize how highly you are thought of in this school. If I had to guess which student did this, the last one I would've thought of would be you. You must give your teacher a heartfelt apology and promise me you will never do anything like that again." I did apologize, but I didn't like it.

By the time I was a senior, my attitude was even lousier. I just wanted to get out of North Dakota and go to California. I had even written my Aunt Clara and Uncle Henry and asked for a classified edition of their paper with jobs available in Encinitas. Nate was already in his second year at Minot State and working there as well.

Lucy's dad had approached my stepfather and said he would pay for my college education if I would just go with Lucy to Minot. At that time, Minot was called "State Teachers' College." I would sometimes later regret I hadn't taken the offer of a free education. It just wasn't in the cards for me.

I worked in the superintendent's office a couple hours a day and came to admire Mr. Killie. He once said, "I know you have not had the easiest life, but when we did the IQ tests, you had the same IQ as another girl in your class who is getting straight As. I think you could do better if you just applied yourself to your classwork."

Because we worked at the *Free Press*, Allen and I had first access to know who the people were at the top of our class. I practically had to wring it out of Allen and called Lucy to tell her she and Bill had tied for valedictorian! Her first comment was, "He really deserves it more than me because he took more difficult classes." Delores was salutatorian, and her sister, Dorothy, ranked third in the class.

Now, you might wonder where I was in the ranks. I told my children for years when they were able to understand that I was seventh in my class. They were very impressed because their high school numbered in the thousands. One day, when he was in the seventh grade, my son, Shane, asked me, "Well, how many were in your class?" I had to admit there were 29!

When I told Mr. Killie I was moving to California, he said, "Oh, I hoped you would stay here. I talked to Judge Whipple, and you can go to work for him in his office. There's also a nice coach coming in next year. Maybe he can take you out."

So much for my plans to get away from my family and go to California. When I announced what my plans were, they decided to go to California also! We sent a few things ahead, after we had an auction sale, and piled in the car—the folks, Sister Candace, Terry (my two-year-old brother), and me!

Kids' Jargon

(Things us kids used to say–usually when the parents weren't around)

1. "What's the matter with you? Are you a communist?"
2. "Boys have two holes in their bodies. Girls have three holes in their bodies."
3. "Liar, liar, pants on fire, tail as long as a telephone wire."
4. "Don't say I never gave you anything." *(Said after sharing piece of candy, etc.)*
5. "Why are you looking at me like I have three heads?"
6. "Jar loose with some of that money." *(Meaning: hand over some cash.)*
7. "Ditto." *(I agree.)*
8. "Up yours!"
9. "See my finger? See my thumb? See my fist? Better run!"
10. "We have other fish to fry." *(More important things to do.)*
11. "Would be better than a sharp stick in the eye."

About the Author

Always writing, Carol Owen Reynolds authors short stories just like many of you play golf, go fishing, or make crafts for your homes. The short stories that preceded her first book, *Stories from a North Dakota Cheerleader*, earned her a letter of congratulations from Governor Doug Burgum after she took a chance and sent him a copy.

Carol's skill at putting thoughts into words was encouraged early on by her high school teacher, Elizabeth Pfeiffer. Later in life, Carol sought creative writing classes at Grossmont College in El Cajon, California.

Her second book, *The Locas: A Collection of Stories about 13 "Crazy Women"*, explores Carol's life before and after a spiritual awakening influenced by a Catholic Cursillo retreat (known in the Protestant faith as the Walk to Emmaus). *Fessenden! Looking Back on a Small-Town North Dakota Life* is her third publication.

Words of encouragement are welcome and may be sent to Jan-Carol Publishing at communications@jancarolpublishing.com.

www.ingramcontent.com/pod-product-compliance
Lightning Source LLC
LaVergne TN
LVHW011052110826
845149LV00015B/3477

9781970471229